EYE ON SPACE

Space Watch: The Earth

Chris Oxlade

PowerKiDS
press.

New York

Published in 2011 by The Rosen Publishing Group Inc.
29 East 21st Street, New York, NY 10010

First Edition

Editor: Julia Adams
Designer: Robert Walster
Picture researcher: Julia Adams

Library of Congress Cataloging-in-Publication Data

Oxlade, Chris.
   Space watch. The Earth / by Chris Oxlade. — 1st ed.
      p. cm. — (Eye on space)
   Includes index.
   ISBN 978-1-61532-540-5 (library binding)
   ISBN 978-1-61532-544-3 (paperback)
   ISBN 978-1-61532-545-0 (6-pack)
   1. Earth—Juvenile literature. I. Title. II. Title: Earth.
   QB631.4.O955 2011
   525—dc22
                                                    2009044670

Photographs:
Alamy: Luiz C. Marigo 20, Reinhard Dirscherl 21;
iStockphoto: 17; NASA: front cover; SOHO/EIT: 10;
NASA/Goddard Space Flight Centre: 9; NASA/JPL-
Caltech/T. Pyle (SSC): 18/19; Shutterstock: Pichugin
Dmitry 1, 7, Stephen Aaron Rees 2, 4, Jonathan Feinstein
5, Anson Hung 2, 6, AridOcean 8, Armin Rose 12,
Alessio Ponti 13, 15; Tudor Photography: 22, 23.
Illustrations: Graham Rich

Manufactured in China
CPSIA Compliance Information: Batch #WAS0102PK: For Further Information
contact Rosen Publishing, New York, New York at 1-800-237-9932

Web Sites

Due to the changing nature of Internet links, PowerKids Press has developed an online list of Web sites related to the subject of this book. This site is updated regularly. Please use this link to access this list:
http://www.powerkidslinks.com/eos/earth

Contents

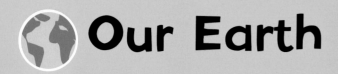 Our Earth

The place were we live is called Earth.

It is made up of land and water.

The water forms oceans, lakes, and rivers.

This is the Atlantic Ocean. Which
sea or ocean is nearest to you?

The Earth's land forms continents.
There are six continents. Do you
know which continent you live on?

This is what the Earth's land
looks like from the sky.

Earth's Features

The Earth has many different landscapes. There are long chains of mountains called mountain ranges. There are wide, flat plains and deep valleys and canyons.

The Grand Canyon in Arizona is 6,230 feet (1,900 m) deep.

Some land is covered with thick forests. Other areas are covered with ice and snow. In some places, there is bare rock or sandy desert.

The Himalayas are the highest mountains in the world

The Earth's Shape

When you look at a map of the Earth, the Earth looks flat. You need to look at a photograph of the Earth from far away to see its shape.

The yellow areas on this map are mountains.

Hundreds of years ago, people thought the Earth was flat.

This is a photograph of the Earth from space. From here, the Earth looks like a big ball. This shape is called a sphere.

Sunlight

The Sun is a huge, glowing ball of fiery hot gas. It is the Earth's closest star. The Sun gives the Earth light and warmth.

The Sun looks like a ball of fire.

Never look straight at the Sun! It can harm your eyes.

The Sun's rays warm the Earth. Some parts of the Earth are closer to the Sun. The rays of the Sun warm these parts up the most.

The hottest part of the Earth is the area around the middle.

Earth

Sun

Different Regions

The Earth has different areas called regions.
The polar regions are at the top and bottom
of the Earth. They are very cold, because
the Sun's rays hardly reach them.

Penguins live in the Antarctic. It is the
polar region at the bottom of the Earth.

The area around the middle of the
Earth is the equatorial region. It is
very hot here all year round.

There are many deserts in the equatorial region.

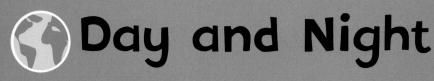 Day and Night

The Earth spins around. This means that the Earth's regions all have daytime and nighttime. It takes the Earth 24 hours to spin around once.

The time it takes the Earth to spin around once is called a day.

Earth

Sun

The Sun lights up one side of the Earth. On this side, it is daytime. On the other side, it is nighttime.

The Sun is shining on this side of the Earth.

Moving around the Sun

The Earth moves around the Sun.

It moves in a giant circle called an orbit.

The Earth moves around the Sun once every 365 days.

The time it takes the Earth to move around the Sun once is called a year.

A year is the time it takes from one birthday to the next.

The Solar System

The Earth is part of a group of planets.
There are eight planets in this group.
Some planets are smaller than the
Earth. Some are much bigger.

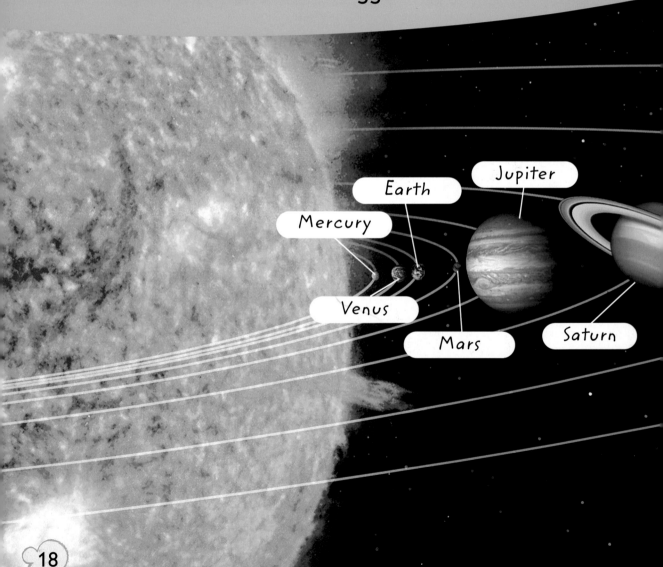

Jupiter

Earth

Mercury

Venus

Mars

Saturn

Together, the planets and the Sun make up the solar system. The Sun is at the center of the solar system.

Uranus

Neptune

Earth is the third planet from the Sun.

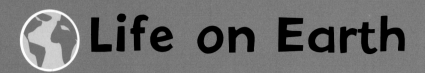 Life on Earth

The Earth is the only planet in the solar system with life. Animals and plants live on the land, in the oceans, and in the air.

Thousands of different animals make their homes in rain forests.

Animals and plants cannot live without water. The Earth is the only planet with water in the solar system.

Many animals live in the deep oceans.

The Earth is a very special place. We must take care of it.

Make a Day and Night Clock

Make a day and night clock to help you practice telling the time.

You will need:
- an empty cereal box
- paintbrush and paints
- 2 paper plates
- 2 paper fasteners
- cardboard • pencil
- colored pens
- glue • scissors

1. Paint one side of a cereal box yellow and the other side black.

2. Glue one plate to each side of the box. Draw a clock face onto each plate.

22

3. Draw two long hands and two short hands onto the cardboard. Cut them out.

4. Use the paper fasteners to attach a long hand and a short hand to each clock face.

5. Paint the Moon and stars on the nighttime side.

6. Paint the Sun and flowers on the daytime clock.

Glossary and Further Information

continent one of the six enormous pieces of land on the Earth

desert a place where it is very dry and there are few plants

map a drawing that shows where things are on the land

plain a very large, flat area of land

ray light or heat traveling in a straight line

region an area of the Earth

Books

Earth
by Christine Taylor-Butler
(Children's Press, 2008)

On Earth
by G. Brian Karas
(Puffin, 2008)

Planet Earth
by Leonie Pratt
(Usborne, 2007)

Index

525 O   HSWCX
Oxlade, Chris.
Space watch.

SOUTHWEST EXPRESS
12/11